MOR *Stories* 4

By Caroline Blakely

Extra stories for each regular lesson in
*Skill Book 4: Other Vowel Sounds and
Consonant Spellings*
in the Laubach Way to Reading series

New Readers Press • Syracuse, New York

ISBN 0-88336-930-3

© 1986, 1991
New Readers Press
Publishing Division of Laubach Literacy
1320 Jamesville Ave., Syracuse, New York 13210

Printed in the United States of America

20   19   18   17   16   15   14   13   12   11
10   9   8   7

To the Teacher

More Stories 4 is a supplementary reader for *Skill Book 4: Other Vowel Sounds and Consonant Spellings* in the Laubach Way to Reading series. It has two or three stories correlated to the new vocabulary and sentence structures taught in each regular lesson of *Skill Book 4*. (Lessons 7 and 11 are review lessons and do not have correlated stories. Review Lesson 16 has one correlated exercise. There are no stories in this book to accompany the correlated reader, *People and Places*.)

These stories are designed as extra reading practice, to reinforce vocabulary and grammatical structures taught in each lesson of *Skill Book 4*. If the students can read independently, they may enjoy and benefit from reading the stories at home. If not, you may help students read the stories in class.

A few exercises are included in place of stories. Students may answer the questions on separate paper or orally.

New words and structures taught in each lesson of *Skill Book 4* are included in the corresponding stories of *More Stories 4*. Thus, the vocabulary in this book has been carefully controlled.

Other new words are listed at the beginning of the story in which they are introduced. The sounds in most of these new words have already been taught, but a few highly useful sight words are introduced. Each new word is used at least three times in the story or the one following.

You should go over the new words with students before they read the story. Have students sound out words that have only sounds previously taught. Tell students the sight words, and have them repeat these words after you.

This book may be used not only with English-speaking students, but also with speakers of other languages who are learning English through the Laubach Way to English series.

Contents

You and the Computer

amazing (u mā′ zing)   program (prō′ gram)
how   reel (rēl)
memory (mem′ or y)   spell

This is the age of computers. These amazing machines touch your life every day. More than one computer has your Social Security number, your name, and your address. These facts tell who you are.

Computers make up many of the bills that you pay each month. A computer keeps facts in its memory bank. It has the facts needed to make up your bill. The computer knows who you are and where you live. The computer's memory knows what you paid on your last bill and what you still have to pay. It knows what other costs have been added. From these records, the computer can tell what you will have to pay this time.

It is amazing that the computer can come up with your bill so fast. It is amazing that the bill is right most of the time. But sometimes computers are not right. One person got a telephone bill for nearly $30,000. He said the computer must not be right. He said he didn't even have a telephone!

Computers can touch your life in more ways than the bills you get. You may have your own computer. And what can you do with your own computer? A lot of things!

For example, you can use a computer to amuse yourself. You may say that you don't like TV games. You like fishing instead. OK, a computer can help you fish.

You can get a computer program that prints up facts on fishing. This program will tell you which fish are in which rivers and lakes. It will tell you what time of the year you can take game fish that are protected by the state. The program will tell you what each kind of fish likes to eat and at what time of day they eat.

Is there any other way that computers can help you fish? Yes, if you want to buy a computer reel. This is a fishing reel with a little computer in it. When a fish hits, the computer reel tells you how far away your line was and how far under the water it was. The reel tells you how fast you were reeling the line in. Then you can do everything the same way again.

If you're fishing in a boat, you may want a fish finder. With the use of a computer, the fish finder can show you what is under the boat. You can see water, grass, mud, and rocks—and even fish.

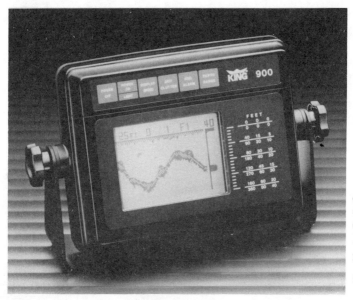

A fish finder

A computer can make a game of learning. You can learn to read better while you have fun. And you can learn to spell better. If you don't spell a word right, the computer will tell you. It will tell you how to spell the word right.

Both you and your children can learn from a computer. A four-year-old may learn letters and some other things she needs to know before she learns to read. She can learn to tell left from right. She can learn to start reading on the left and follow a line over to the right.

Computers can help teachers do a better job. A computer can help a teacher keep up with what each person in the class has learned. Then the teacher knows the needs of each person.

Yes, this is the computer age. Make the most of it. Computers won't cure everything that isn't right in your life. But a computer may save enough time for you to do the rest.

Computer Jobs

average (av′ er ij)
data (dā′ tu)
input (in′ put)
instructions (in struc′ shunz)
operate (op′ er ate)
operator (op′ er ā tor)
payroll (pay′ rōll)
programmer (prō gram er)

out
school
skill
step
tape

In many businesses, computers are opening up new jobs for people. Computers can't think. People have to think for them and put facts and instructions into the computer in a form it can read.

Kinds of computer jobs

For example, let's say that a company wants the computer to do its payroll.

The computer programmer. First, a program must be written for that job. The computer programmer writes this plan. It tells the computer and the other workers what they have to do.

To write the program, the programmer thinks of the facts in the computer's memory that are needed for this job. These may be the names, addresses, and Social Security numbers of every worker. Then, the programmer thinks of other data (facts) that will be needed. One fact needed is the time that each worker has put in for this payroll. Other facts may be needed, like the pay for each worker and overtime pay.

The computer can compute how much tax to take out and how much pay each worker has gotten up to date, but the program must give instructions for doing these things.

The programmer must think of every step the computer must follow. Then the programmer must put the steps in the right order. He or she must write the instructions for the computer to follow. The programmer must write the instructions for the other workers, too.

Data input workers. After the program is written and tested, data input workers put the needed facts in a form that the computer can read. (There are sometimes other names for these workers.)

Data input workers may put holes in computer cards. Each hole stands for a letter or a number or an instruction. Or the data input workers may put the data on tapes or some other input form.

The computer operator. When the programmer and the data input workers have done their jobs, the computer operator takes over. He or she loads the computer with the needed input data (cards, tapes, or other forms). Then the operator watches while the computer is running. Lights come on if the computer isn't running right. If that happens, the operator stops the computer and checks the program instructions. Sometimes, the operator will bring the programmer in to check the program. Sometimes, the operator will phone for someone to repair the computer.

Other jobs. After the computer does its job, other workers are needed. They run the printer and do other jobs to make the print-out from the computer ready for the department that ordered the job. (In the example we have used, that is the payroll department.)

On the job

Most computers are in nice business offices. So computer workers work in nice places. Computers won't work where it is very hot or very cold. So computer workers don't work in hot or cold places. Some businesses run their computers day and night every day of the week. So some computer workers work at night or on weekends. Many data input workers work part-time.

Getting the job

Sometimes, office workers who run other office machines become computer workers. But most computer workers have studied computer skills in school. Most programmers finish college. Many high schools and colleges teach computer skills. Other schools teach nothing but computer skills.

In 1986, there were 1,188,000 computer jobs. There will be many more jobs by the year 2000. There will be more jobs for programmers, operators, and those who work with the print-out from the computer. There won't be as many jobs for data input workers. Computers won't be as hard to use. Many kinds of workers will be able to put in data.

In 1986, computer operators made an average of $16,500 a year. Data input workers averaged $11,600 to $18,300 a year. Computer programmers averaged $27,000 a year.

Hugh Writes to His Sister

about   blue   our

Dear Ann,

You missed a lot of fun last weekend at the family reunion. At first, I argued about going and even refused to go. Then, I went to please Mother.

The reunion was at the home of Aunt Mary and Uncle John. You know what a great view they have of Lake Huron. Mother and Dad and I went on Friday to help get things ready.

About 30 relatives came on Saturday for the big barbecue. I haven't seen some of them since Jack's wedding. By the way, Jack and Joan were there from Texas with our three-year-old niece, Pam. They hope to see you before they drive back to Texas.

Grandmother and Grandfather King were there. They came from Florida by airplane. They asked about your first year at college. Mother was happy to tell about you, and she continues to show everyone your latest pictures.

I was afraid of being the only teenager there. But a few of our cousins came from Canada. One of Uncle John's nephews is my age. We had fun.

You know how much Aunt Ellen and Dad like to argue. Well, they started arguing while Aunt Ellen was eating some barbecued ribs. She choked and her face turned blue. A piece of meat was stuck in her throat. She was not able to breathe.

I remembered seeing a sign that told what to do when a person is choking. I got behind her and made a fist of my right hand right under her ribs. Then I gave her a big hug, pressing hard against my fist with my left hand. Up came the piece of meat, and Aunt Ellen breathed again.

That was my first rescue of the day. Later, I rescued little Pam from the lake. The children were playing on the shore. The water isn't over their heads there. But a big wave came and carried Pam out over her head. I got to her first and lifted her out of the waves. She was afraid and choking on water. But she was not hurt.

Well, that tells you how your "little brother" was "big man" at the family reunion. Aren't you glad I was there? I am. We have an OK family.

Write and tell me about college life. We are waiting for you to come home next month.

Your brother,

Hugh

Hug for Life

attack (u tack')   Heimlich (Hīm' lik)
heart (hart)   now

Many people die each year from choking. But not as many people die as in the past. People now know what to do when a person is choking. Now they know how to hug a person in the right way, so that air brings the object out of the person's throat.

This way of saving a choking person's life was started in 1974. Dr. Heimlich told how to do it. Since then, the Heimlich hug has saved many people from choking.

The Heimlich hug is not hard to do. Even children can do it, so many schools teach it. About 20 states say eating places must put up signs that show how to do the Heimlich hug. Some other countries have programs that teach the Heimlich hug and when to use it.

A choking person will die in four minutes if he doesn't get help. There isn't time for a doctor to get to him. Someone near must save the choking person.

Is it choking or a heart attack?

In order to be able to save someone, you have to *know* that he is choking. Sometimes a choking person dies when the people near him think that he is having a heart attack.

That doesn't have to happen. There are ways to tell a choking person from one having a heart attack.

- If the person is a child, he is likely to be choking. Few children have heart attacks.
- If a person is eating, or in an eating place, he is likely to be choking.
- If a person is not able to speak, he is likely to be choking. A person having a heart attack can speak.

The signs of choking

1. The person cannot breathe or speak.
2. The person turns blue.
3. The person passes out.

If you see someone that you think is choking, ask her or him. If the person is choking, she won't be able to speak. But she may be able to give a sign with her head or hand.

If the person has passed out before you get to him or her, you can still save a life. Ask these questions of yourself: Is the person breathing? Is the person blue in the face? Are there signs that the person was eating something?

If the answer to these questions is yes, you may save a life. But you must act fast.

What to do

1. Stand behind the choking person.
2. Make a fist with one of your hands.
3. Put your fist just below the person's ribs.
4. With your other hand, press your fist in and up quickly. Press hard enough so that air comes up. This will bring the object up from the person's throat.
5. The object may come up after you press the first time. But you may have to press again and again.

Answering Ads

hello (hel ō)

Kitty O'Toole is looking for an apartment. She reads the ads in the paper about apartments for rent. Then she tries some of the telephone numbers given in the ads. First, she tries 426-3530.

Kitty: Hello. I'm Kitty O'Toole. I'm answering your ad in last night's paper.

Woman: Hello, Kitty, I'm Kay Smith. Are you looking for a furnished apartment? That's what I have. I'm looking for a roommate to share the cost of rent and utilities.

Kitty: Can you use two roommates? My friend, Jane Hoover, and I are looking for a place together. We are both quiet, and we don't smoke.

Woman: No. You sound nice. But this is a two-bedroom apartment. There's room for just one other person.

Kitty: That's too bad. Your place is near where I work. Thanks anyway. I'll keep looking.

*   *   *

Next, Kitty rings 427-8060 and speaks into the telephone.

Kitty: Hello. Do you still have the four-room apartment for rent on Circle Drive?

Man: Yes. How soon do you want to move in?

Kitty: Well, I want to look at it first. May my friend and I come to see it on Sunday afternoon?

Man: Yes, but it may be rented before then. I can't save it for anyone if I don't get a deposit. This is a nice place—four large, unfurnished rooms for three hundred dollars. I pay the heat and other utilities.

Kitty: It sounds about right for us. I can come to see it at noon today. Which bus do I take from the center of the city?

Man: Take the university bus to Circle Drive. Then turn right past three apartment buildings. Mine is the fourth building. I live in Apartment 3 on the first floor. My name is John Gates.

Kitty: My name is Kitty O'Toole. I'll see you soon, Mr. Gates. By the way, there isn't a swimming pool in the building, is there?

Man: No. But some people use the university pools.

Kitty: That sounds great. I'll see you about noon.

The Rights and Duties of a Renter

because	lease (lēs)
bug	legal (lē' gul)
duty (dū' ty)	receipt (rē sēt')

You are a renter. What are your rights and duties?

● Before you sign a lease, look at the apartment with the landlord. See if any repairs are needed. Write them on a piece of paper and keep them. Even if the landlord doesn't agree to make the repairs, he needs to know the repairs were needed *before* you moved in.

● If you feel that the landlord refused to rent to you because of your color, race, or sex, or because you are handicapped, you have a right to protest. Go to the Human Rights office in your city. It's possible that you can take the landlord to court.

● It is your duty to keep records that show you paid the rent and security deposit. Keep the receipt that the landlord gives you when you pay the rent. Keep the receipt you get for the security deposit. It is better to pay by check or money order. Then, if you can't find the receipt, you still have a record of paying.

- Don't stop paying the rent in order to make a landlord repair the place. The landlord can make you move for doing that. The only time it is legal not to pay the landlord is when you take the rent money to a legal office. The legal office will give the money to the landlord after he makes the repairs.

- If your apartment is the only one in the building that has bugs, it is your duty to kill the bugs. If other apartments in the building have bugs, it is the landlord's duty to kill them.

- It is your duty to keep the apartment looking much as it did when you moved in.

- Your first right as a renter is to be left alone in the peace and quiet of your home.

- You have the right to work with other renters in order to stand up for your rights.

The Rights and Duties of a Landlord

code

You are a landlord. What are your rights and duties?

● When you rent out a place to live, you must not turn away any person because of color, race, sex, or because of a handicap.

● Renters in apartment buildings can put on their own locks, but the landlord has a right to a key.

● You have a right to go into a rented apartment to make repairs or to show the place to someone who may rent or buy it. This does not mean that you can go into the place any time you please. You own the building, but it is your renter's home. You cannot tell him again and again to do things, like keeping the place clean.

● You have the right to make a renter move if he doesn't pay the rent and if he doesn't do what the lease says. This is a legal matter. You have to go to court to make the renter move.

- Sometimes you have the right to lock a renter out of an apartment. You may want to lock furniture in, or you may want to put everything out on the street. Before you do something like this, you need to ask at a legal office if you have the right to do so.

- You have a duty to make some repairs on the building. You have to make any repairs that your lease says you will. It is your duty to know the building code of the city. Sometimes you have to make repairs to pass the code. If your building doesn't pass the code, the city can take you to court.

- It is your duty to keep the building safe for your renters. If your renter is hurt because of something you didn't do, he can take you to court.

- You must let your renter alone. It is his home. You must let him live in peace.

This Is Canada

Arctic (Arc' tic)
Atlantic (At lan' tic)
important (im por' tunt)
Ottawa (Ot' u wu)
Pacific (Pu sif' ic)

ocean (ō' shun)
province (prov' ins)
east
west
wheat

Canada is the largest country in North America. It is the second largest country in the world. This large country is north of the United States. Canada and the United States have been friends for many years.

Canada is large, but it has few people. There are some big cities. But a lot of the country is covered with trees, high hills, and lakes. In the far north, it is very, very cold for most of the year. Very few people live there.

There are oceans on three sides of Canada. The Atlantic Ocean is on the east. The Pacific Ocean is on the west. The Arctic Ocean is on the north. With so much water near, many people fish for a living.

Trees cover about a third of Canada. Many of the trees are cut to make paper. Canada makes more paper than any other country.

There are not many trees or hills in the center of Canada. That is where the first people in North America lived. They were Indians who lived by hunting and fishing. There are great wheat farms there now. Wheat is used to make bread and breakfast food. Wheat is Canada's most important crop. Apples are an important crop, too. They grow in the west near the Pacific Ocean.

There are 10 provinces in Canada. A province is like a state in the United States. But most of Canada's provinces are larger than states in the U.S. The far north country near the Arctic Ocean is a part of Canada, but it is not a province. This Arctic country is very, very cold with ice and snow most of the year.

Canada became a free country in 1931. But it continues to have ties to the mother country. The English queen is still honored as Canada's head of state.

Margaret Myers

Ottawa is the capital city. Ottawa is in the east. Ottawa is not far from the Atlantic Ocean.

Canada's flag is red and white. It has a red maple leaf on a white stripe. On both sides of the maple leaf are red stripes.

Family life in Canada is much like that in the United States. People eat many kinds of food. They eat English and French dishes. But they eat fast food like hamburgers, too. Some of the people speak English. Some speak French. French is the language for many people in provinces in the east.

Every province in Canada has a lot of snow in the cold months. Ice hockey is a top sport. So are other ice and snow sports.

Schools are important to people in Canada. Many children start school when they are four or five years old. They have to go to school from age 6 to 16. Many go to high school for five years.

Canada is a nation of many faces. You can see Arctic families living in homes made of ice. But you can see people in high city apartments, too, eating the best French dishes. You can see farmers and factory workers and hockey players and students. These are just a few of the faces of Canada. There are many others. And if you visit Canada, you'll find that most of them are friendly.

July Fun Days

sunny   three-legged

It was Sunday, July 3. Dan Porter met the 10 o'clock plane from Florida. His two children, Carl and Gail, were going to spend the week with him. After many kisses and hugs, they started driving back to Center City.

"What shall we do today?" asked Dan. "The zoo opens up today. Do you want to go there?"

"I love zoos," said Gail. "Let's go."

After an afternoon at the petting zoo, the three of them went to Big J's for hamburgers. "I don't know about you, but I'm tired," said Dan. "Let's go home and watch TV awhile and then go to bed. We have a lot to do on the Fourth of July holiday."

The next morning was sunny and bright. "It's a fine day for a parade," said Carl. "Let's hurry and eat breakfast. I don't want to miss anything."

By 10 o'clock, the three Porters were waiting on Main Street for the parade. "Here it comes," yelled Carl. "I see the flag leading the way. I hear the drums and the flutes, and the bugles. They are playing 'The Stars and Stripes Forever.' "

"That music makes me feel like crying," said Gail.

"That's no way to honor your flag," said her brother. "Hold your head up high, and put your hand over your heart when the flag goes by."

"And don't you forget to remove your hat before you salute," said Gail.

The Porters followed the parade up Main Street to Jones Park. There they had a picnic lunch and watched the bicycle races. In the games that followed, Carl and Gail won a prize in the three-legged race. Then, as it was getting dark, they watched the fireworks.

"May we go to the band concert at 9 o'clock?" asked Carl. "It's at Lake Shore Park. Is that far?"

"No, it's not far. We can go," said Dan. "We'll be tired. But we can sleep late in the morning. Come on. Let's go."

Dan and his children had fun the rest of the evening and the rest of the week. They went to the car races. They went to see a play. They went to the country club for dinner. On Thursday evening, Dan had a sign language class. Gail and Carl liked that, too. On Friday, they went to a barbecue put on by the Valley Fire Department. They spent Saturday at a band concert.

Then it was Sunday, the day that the children had to return to Florida and their mother. Dan put them on the plane. Dan felt both sad and happy. He felt sad because they were going away from him. But he was happy that they had had so much fun for a week.

Judy's Diary

diary (dī' u ry)   peaceful

Judy writes in her diary every night. Her diary is a kind of record of her life. She tells what happened that day. She tells her feelings, as well as facts. This is what she wrote in her diary last Thursday.

Thursday, June 30

Today was a very hot day. The heat made us feel like arguing. Luke refused to eat his dinner. Lewis yelled at him to eat. Then he ate so fast that I was afraid he was going to choke. I yelled at him to chew his meat. Then Luke cried so hard that he threw up. Oh well, there's no rule that every family dinner has to be peaceful.

After dinner, we sat out on the steps to get some cool air. Everyone was quiet. Little Luke was still thinking about the yelling. I was, too, and I wanted to hug my sad little boy. I didn't because Lewis doesn't like for me to "baby" our four-year-old son. Lewis grew up thinking a boy has to act like a man. And it's true that Lewis had to be the man in the family after his father died. But I like to have a little boy to hug. Luke will be a man soon enough.

Lewis has had a hard life. But some of it has been in his own mind. When a person grows up poor, he is afraid it is because his family didn't try hard enough. That may be true sometimes. But that wasn't true of Lewis's family. His father and mother worked hard when they came to this country. In fact, Lewis's father worked so hard that he died young. He didn't leave his family any money. But he did a lot to make Lewis the man he is today.

Lewis works hard on the public works crew. It's a hard, dirty job. Lewis gets tired, but he can take it. We are far from rich. But there's enough money so that I can stay home with the boys. Both of us think that's important right now. We do get a little tired of leftovers. Things will change after the boys start school. Lewis thinks he doesn't want his wife to work, but he may change his mind.

Lewis still has the dream of giving me fine clothes and jewels. They're not important to me. I'm happy with my husband and my boys. But if Lewis gets me jewels, I'll wear them just to make him happy.

Emergency Phoning

basement (base' ment)   flush

Carmen Lopez is angry. She has just looked at an apartment. The landlord told her it was rented. Carmen knows the apartment is not rented yet. Carmen is phoning the Human Rights office to report this matter.

Human Rights Officer: Hello. Human Rights. I'm Officer Miller. Can I help you?

Lopez: Yes. A landlord has refused to rent me an apartment this morning. It's because I come from Mexico. My name is Carmen Lopez.

Miller: Did this happen here in the city?

Lopez: Yes. The apartment is on Green Street.

Miller: How do you know the apartment wasn't rented when you looked at it?

Lopez: My friend phoned the landlord five minutes before I went to look at the apartment. It was not rented. My friend does not speak as I do. She has lived in this city most of her life. That's why I asked her to phone for me.

Miller: Can you come to our office today? It's in the Public Office Building on State Street. We're on the fourth floor. We can meet with you at 3:00 p.m.

Lopez: Yes, I'll be there. Can you do something about this matter?

Miller: We'll try. But first, we have to make a report. If you'll give us the information, we'll write it up and make the report. And before you come this afternoon, I'll go over and try to rent that place. You said it was Green Street?

Lopez: Yes, 303 Green Street, Apartment 7, and you'll find the landlord in Apartment 1. Thanks a lot. I'll be at your office at 3:00.

* * *

Molly's sewer line is stopped up. Water is standing on the floor of her basement. The basement is under her first floor apartment. Molly phones the department of public works (DPW) in this emergency.

Molly: Hello. This is Molly Hoover at 1400 Oak Street. Can you send someone to flush out my sewer line?

DPW: Have we flushed out your sewer line before?

Molly: Yes, you flushed it out about this time last year.

DPW: Is water standing in the basement?

Molly: Yes, my basement floor is covered with water.

DPW: Well, it sounds like an emergency. We'll be there about 9:00 a.m. But if there are tree roots in the sewer line, flushing won't help. We'll do what we can.

The Job of a Trash Collector

collect (col ect')   outside (out side)
collector (col ect' er)   shovel (shuv' ul)

Trash collectors work for the department of public works or for a trash collecting company. They go with big trucks to pick up the trash on every street. Sometimes they use shovels to clean the streets.

Trash collectors empty the trash cans and throw trash bags into the trucks. Sometimes they have to work the lifts that pack trash into the truck. They may have to shovel snow into trucks. They may have to shovel rocks or leaves into trucks.

To get this job, you have to be able to lift heavy loads. You have to be willing to work outside when it is raining or snowing or when it is very hot. You don't have to have much schooling or pass any kind of test. But you do have to be willing to work hard.

Trash collectors are not paid as well as others in the public works department. The pay changes a lot from place to place—more than that of any other workers. In 1986, the pay was from $8,000 to $21,000 a year. Trash collectors get paid holidays and sick days. They get pay when they retire. Some of them become truck drivers, but most do not go on to a better job.

To get this job, you must make application to the department of public works or to a company that collects trash.

There will continue to be a lot of jobs for trash collectors to the year 2000.

Duke Gets a Job

interview (in′ ter view)
personnel (per son el′)

Duke has a job interview. He goes to the personnel office of the *Oak Park News.* He asks for the personnel officer. When a man comes into the room, Duke stands up and holds out his hand.

Duke: Hello! I'm Duke Miller. I have an interview for a job on the paper. I filled out an application yesterday. I read in the ads that you have an opening. I hope it's in the sports department. I'd be a great sports writer.

Personnel officer: Hello, Duke. I was expecting you. My name is Joe Oliver. We do have an opening. But it's not writing news. The main duty is to load newspapers onto trucks. But before we go into that, I have to know how old you are. I can't use anyone under 18.

Duke: I was 18 on my last birthday. That was in January. And I finished high school last Tuesday. Now that I'm not a student, I'm ready to bring home some big bucks.

Mr. Oliver: Well, the bucks may not be so big, but they will come every week. You look as if you can lift heavy loads. How are you at math? The person doing this job has to keep records of papers going out and coming in. That takes math.

Duke: I was stupid in math before I met Mr. Newman. He works here in the press room. I knew him from church camp. He was the sports coach there. When I told him I was going to drop out of school, he tutored me in math. He knew how to make me understand. Now, I can do math.

Mr. Oliver: I believe you, but you'll have to take a little test anyway. How are you at getting up at 5:00 a.m.?

Duke: I get up before that when I go fishing with my dad.

Mr. Oliver: I've learned a lot about your interests and skills in this short interview. You seem to be a go-getter. If you do OK on the math test, the job is yours.

Duke: Great! When do I start?

Mr. Oliver: I'll telephone you tonight, and the job starts on Wednesday at 5:00 a.m. I see from your application that you live on Fourth Avenue. Getting to work won't be hard for you.

Duke: No, I'll ride my bicycle the first few weeks. Then I'll have enough money saved to buy some better wheels.

Mr. Oliver: You seem to know what you want. Here's the math test. You can sit at this table. When you finish, give the test to the young lady over there.

Duke: Thanks for the interview, Mr. Oliver. I'll hope to hear from you tonight.

Jobs for Teenagers

certificate (ser tif' i cut)	gas
deliver (dē liv er)	hour
experience (ex pēr' ē ens)	power
	wash

Most of us get our first job when we are teenagers. Teenage jobs are important. They are a kind of school for the world of work. Teenagers get experience in working. And they get experience in spending or saving the pay they get.

Finding a job

If you are a teenager and want a job, how do you find one? First, ask your friends and family about jobs. Read the help wanted ads in the newspaper. Check out jobs in places you know about, like food stores, fast food places, or car wash services.

Go to these businesses and put in an application. If you have any kind of work experience—such as baby-sitting, cutting grass, or carrying newspapers—put that on your application.

Speak to the personnel officer, or the person who gives the jobs. That person may not have a job opening now. But if he needs help later, he'll remember that you were interested.

Many cities have job centers for teenagers. Workers in these job centers can tell you about job openings. Many centers have computers to keep up with jobs. The computers tell where the jobs are, what they pay, and what skills you need to get these jobs.

Many of these centers help young people find jobs in city or state services, like parks and public works. Some are jobs in the months that school is out. Some are on-the-job training programs where teenagers work part-time and go to school part-time.

Teenagers are protected

There was a time when children and teenagers were used for cheap labor. They worked many hours for very little money. Now there are rules that protect young people. These rules must be followed in order for teenagers to have jobs.

If you're 14 or 15. Most states say you must be 14 to have a job. If you're under 16, you cannot work in school hours. You cannot work more than three hours on school days or eight hours a day on other days. Here are some jobs you can do if you're 14 or 15.

- Office work; operating office machines.
- Store jobs; taking money for sales or services; marking prices, filling orders, packing, bagging, and carrying out orders.
- Delivering things that people buy, but not by driving.
- Clean-up work; operating floor-cleaning machines; shoveling snow or trash, but not operating machines to cut grass.
- Kitchen work; operating machines to wash dishes or make coffee; waiting on tables, clean-up.
- Service to cars; selling gas; putting gas in cars; cleaning and washing cars.

Most states say you cannot work in a factory if you're under 16. You cannot operate power machines.

If you're 16 or 17. When you become 16, you can do many other jobs. But you have to be 18 to drive a car on the job or to use most power machines. You may not be able to work evening or night hours.

If you're 18 or older. You are not under child labor rules after you become 18. You can work at any job you can get and keep.

Working papers

The business that gives you a job has to know that you are the legal age for the job. You have to give the personnel officer an age certificate. You may know this as a work permit or working papers.

Anyone under the age of 18 must have an age certificate in order to get a job. Most of the time, schools give out age certificates. To get an age certificate, telephone the office of the top person in your city's schools. You can get information about getting your age and work certificate.

Social Security card

Like any other worker, the teenager needs a Social Security card. You can get an application for a Social Security number from the nearest Social Security office.

Remember that this will be your Social Security number for life. You will get two cards. Take care of them. Put one with the I.D. papers you carry with you. Put the other card with important family papers like birth certificates.

Life in Early America

danger (dān' jer)
early (er' ly)
fireplace (fire' place)
fort
homemade (home made)

inside (in side)
land
log
plaything (play' thing)
settler (set' ler)

Life was hard for early settlers in America. The first settlers came in boats from the other side of the Atlantic Ocean. That took two to four months. Many of the people were sick when they arrived. Then they had to face the danger of living in a new country.

Indians lived on the land that the settlers came to. Some Indians were friendly. But others were angry that white men were taking over Indian land. To protect themselves, the settlers would build a fort of heavy logs. On each corner, the settlers put guns.

Inside the fort, the settlers made log cabins for families to live in. They lived in the fort for the first winter. Then they needed more land on which to plant crops. Before they could plant, the settlers had to get the land ready. They cut trees and pushed the logs together to be burned. Bushes and roots were pulled up and burned. The families worked together on this hard job. After the crops were planted, there was not so much danger of running out of food.

The settlers didn't have to grow everything they ate. The woods were full of wild animals and birds. The waters were full of fish. They watched the Indians catch fish in the brooks. No hook was needed. The Indians just hit a fish with a stick and pulled it out.

Every cabin had a fireplace. It was made of stones and hard mud. Its burning logs gave heat to keep the cabin warm. Since there were no stoves, meals were cooked on the open fire of the fireplace. Since there were no matches, the family took care not to let the fire go out.

Nearly everything the family needed was made at home. There was no sugar. So the settler made maple sugar from maple trees. There were no stores from which to buy dolls or other playthings. So someone in the family carved doll faces or animals from wood. Some of these homemade playthings were very beautiful.

Life was hard for these early settlers, but they had good times, too. When a family needed a new home, people far and near were asked to help. Women cooked a big dinner while the men put up the sides of the home. After that, the man could finish the home alone. After working hard, everyone had a big party with much eating and drinking.

The first settlers came to the Atlantic shores in 1607. Step by step, in fact many steps on foot, these men and women pushed their way west. In 200 years, some settlers had arrived on the Pacific shores.

This is one chapter in American life. Some of you may think theirs was the good life. Others are glad to be living in a world of TV and computers. One thing can be said about the early settlers. Our nation would not be what it is today if they had not led the way.

Using the Library

library (lī' brār y)   loan
librarian (lī brār' ē un)   subject (sub' ject)

Do you know about the many services you can get at your public library at no cost?

Every library has books on a lot of subjects. These libraries will loan books to people. You can keep a book for two or three weeks.

To take books out of the library, you must get a library card. This helps the library to know where each book is and to find books if people don't bring them back. There is no cost for the card or for the loan of a book. But if you don't return the book on time, you will have to pay a fine. And it is understood that you will pay for the book if you don't bring it back.

When you go to a library, you can get help in finding what you want. You may not know the title of the book you want or the name of the writer. The librarian can help you look for books on that subject. Sometimes you only want a little information, like the date of Mother's Day next year. By looking at the table of contents in the right book, the librarian can help you find just about any information. Librarians are glad to help you in these ways.

If you just need a little information, you may not have to go to the library in person. Many libraries have a number you can use to get information over the phone.

Sally Rubadeau

For some people, it is hard to get to the library. So many big libraries have little libraries in vans. They drive to apartment buildings and other places where many people live.

Books are only a part of what a public library has for the public. You can find music or book records, as well as newspapers. You can use the copy machine for only a few cents. Many libraries loan beautiful pictures to the people with library cards. And many libraries have computers that people can use. You will find programs that are open to the public, too, like storytelling for children and picture shows on many subjects.

If you haven't visited your library lately, why not do it now? It will make your life richer.

Starting a Neighborhood Group

afraid (u fraid')   inner (in' er)
dog   robber (rob' er)

Do you live in a neighborhood in the inner-city? Many neighborhoods in the inner-city have problems. A lot of people are out of work. People are afraid of robbers and groups of young people on the streets. People are afraid of dogs running free. And people are even afraid of their neighbors.

Housing is one of the biggest problems in the inner-city. Not too many years ago, there were fine houses in this part of the city. Then some of the richer home owners moved out to the country. They rented their city homes to poorer persons. Many owners stopped making repairs on the houses. Many of the owners stopped paying taxes, and, after a time, the city took over these old houses. The renters moved out, and the houses were left empty.

Now, these empty houses make the neighborhood look bad. Grass and bushes grow high around the houses. Children throw rocks, and the windows are broken. Children or other people start fires in the empty houses. Sometimes people without homes sleep there. People are afraid to live near these houses.

Does this sound like your neighborhood? Are there many old empty houses near you? Is there trash around the streets and grounds? Do dogs run free in the neighborhood? Do you get little help when you phone the dogcatcher? Do you need more help from the police in protecting your neighborhood from robbers?

If you answer yes to these questions, it may be time for you to do something about your neighborhood.

Yes, you can do something—but not alone. You need to meet with your neighbors to form a neighborhood group. Sometimes, four or five neighborhoods that have problems can work together.

Some neighborhood groups have been able to get some money from a church or from the United Way. This makes it possible to have an office and a telephone and sometimes full-time workers. That's great, but the most important thing is to have six or eight persons who are interested and willing to share that interest with others. This will be the neighborhood council. It is the duty of this council to interest others by word-of-mouth or the written word. Then future members can meet to discuss what needs to be done and what problem they should work on first.

Neighborhood groups of this kind have made some great changes by working together. They have made city leaders listen to their problems and act on them. In many cities, run-down neighborhoods are paying taxes as high as those in rich neighborhoods. A group of inner-city people together can fight this practice.

If you don't have a neighborhood group in your city, you may want to start one. You and your friends, working together, can make your neighborhood better. You will be proud of it and of yourselves.

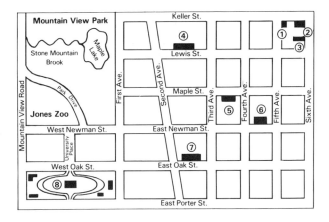

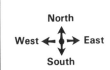

North

West ← ↕ → East

South

Key to Public Buildings

1. City Office Building
2. Courthouse
3. City Jail
4. School Board Office
5. Neighborhood Center
6. Social Security Office
7. South High School
8. Cook University

More Questions about a City Map

Study this map of Mountain City and the key to public buildings. Then answer these questions.

1. Is Third Ave. east or west of Fourth Ave.?
2. Does Mountain View Road run north and south or east and west?
3. What street is the School Board Office on?
4. What public building is found on East Newman St.?
5. Where is the Courthouse?
6. If someone at South High School asked you how to get to the School Board Office, what would you tell him?
7. If someone asked you how to get to the zoo from the Neighborhood Center, what would you say?
8. Is the city jail on Fifth or Sixth Ave.?

Sue Writes to Her Friend Pam

Wednesday, August 1

Dear Pam,

I have the greatest idea! How would you like to spend the last week of the summer with us? That's when the Howard County Fair will be going on in Johnstown. It's the most exciting time of the year around here.

The Browns did OK last year at the fair. I won first place with my horse Sugar. My father was so proud he shouted. Mother's yellow roses got a blue ribbon in the flower show. Dad won the tractor-pulling contest. One of the farmers he drove against held the state record.

Tom won only third prize with his cow Beauty. He was so unhappy that he frowned for hours. This year he thinks it will be easy for Beauty to win a red or blue ribbon.

Have you ever been to a county fair? It's not just horses and cows and contests. There are a lot of exciting rides and games, too. And the clowns are so funny. We'll go to a rock concert, too. The Main Machine is going to be here.

Tell your mother that my mother will be very glad to have you the week before school starts.

We only have a few weeks to make plans. So hurry up and write.

Love,
Sue

Measuring Length and Distance

distance (dis' tuns)   length
front (frunt)   measure (mezh' hur)
inch   yard

Sometimes you want to measure the length of something. Length is measured in inches, feet, yards, and sometimes the three of them. For example, let's say you have a broken window. You measure the window and find that it is 18 inches one way and 30 inches the other way. You tell the salesperson that you need a piece of glass 18 by 30 inches. The length of boards is measured in feet. Many boards are eight feet in length. Some are 12 or 20 feet in length.

The length of some things is measured by yards. You may buy two or three yards of cotton goods to make a dress. In fact, we know goods of this kind as yard goods.

Distance may be measured by feet, yards, or miles. The distance from one city to another is measured in miles. The distance run in a race may be measured in miles or yards. Feet and inches are used in sports contests like the high jump.

You'll find that you need to measure length and distance from time to time. Using the chart below, find the answer to the problems on the following page.

12 inches = 1 foot
3 feet = 1 yard
36 inches = 1 yard
5,280 feet = 1 mile
1,760 yards = 1 mile

Problems in measuring length and distance

1. Ed Brown went 92 feet in the tractor-pulling contest. Was that a little over 30 yards or a little over 40 yards?

2. The pup tent that Sue and Pam are going to sleep in is 36 inches high in front and 24 inches high in back. How many feet high is it in front? How many feet high is it in back?

3. Sue is making a May basket for her sick neighbor. After filling the basket with flowers, she wants to tie a ribbon around it. If it takes 16 inches of ribbon to go around the basket and 20 inches to tie it, how many yards of ribbon will she have to buy?

4. Sue and Pam are making a pie. They need a 10-inch pie pan. They aren't sure if the pan they have is a 10-inch pan. How do they find out?

5. Tom is on a running team at school. Tom gets tired when he tries the mile run. He likes the 100-yard run because it is shorter. How many times would he have to run 100 yards in order to run a mile?

Answers:
1. 30 yards
2. 3 feet in front; 2 feet in back
3. 1 yard
4. Measure the pan from side to side
5. Nearly 18 times

Things Americans Do in a Day

chicken (chick' un)   pound
crash   ton (tun)

Do you like numbers? Tom Parker does, too. He worked five years to find out a lot of information about Americans. Then he wrote a book with the title *In One Day*. It is about the things Americans do in one day and how many Americans do them. Here is some information from Parker's book.

1. Americans spend $700 million a day for fun.
2. Americans throw away 200,000 tons of good food each day. (A ton is 2,000 pounds.) This is food that someone could eat.
3. Americans drink 28 million six-packs of beer each day.
4. About 4,100 Americans have heart attacks each day. And 2,700 die each day of heart problems.
5. Americans buy 50,000 new television sets each day; 30,000 of them are color sets.
6. Americans print 125 new books each day.
7. The police arrest 28,000 people each day. These people would fill 500 buses; 7,000 of the arrests have to do with drinking too much.
8. Four hundred eight Americans are listed as missing persons each day. Of these, 391 are found.
9. Twenty thousand people write a letter to the U.S. president each day.
10. Americans smoke more than 86 million packs of cigarettes each day.
11. Fourteen thousand Americans drop out of high school each day.

12. Americans eat 170 million eggs each day and 12 million chickens.
13. Animal centers kill 30,000 cats and dogs each day because they aren't wanted by anyone.
14. At any one time, there are more than 9 billion bills in paper money. That would be 40 bills for each American.
15. Americans buy 25,000 new cars each day. About 6,000 of them are made in another country.
16. Thirty Americans become 100 years old each day.
17. Americans eat 12.5 million pounds of cheese each day.
18. Six hundred Americans try to kill themselves each day, and 70 *do* kill themselves.
19. Dogs and cats give birth to 70,000 new dogs and cats each day.
20. Americans write 100 million checks each day. A million of them are no good.
21. Fifty thousand Americans crash in their cars every day. Five thousand people are hurt in those crashes. More than 120 Americans die every day in those crashes. Twenty-five of them would have been saved by air bags.

Another Ending to the Dog Story

control (con trōl')   maybe (may' be)
daytime (day' time)   silver (sil' ver)
gone (gawn)

Jerry Dawson is angry about the dog next door. It is a big dog with long claws. It digs holes in Jerry's lawn. First, Jerry tells his neighbor, Bob Shaw, who owns the dog. Then Jerry phones the city animal control department. This is what is said:

Officer: Hello! This is Animal Control.

Jerry: I want to report a dog that comes into my yard and digs holes in my lawn.

Officer: Do you know who owns the dog?

Jerry: Yes, my neighbor, Bob Shaw, owns it. I spoke to him, and he says he's awfully sorry, but it's a strong dog. He says he can't keep it from digging a hole under the fence so it can crawl in my yard. Isn't it against the law for him to let that happen?

Officer: Yes, it is. We'll pay a visit to Mr. Shaw. He will just have to tie up the dog. The next time it comes in your yard, Shaw will have to pay a fine.

Jerry: OK, thanks. I'm glad you can help.

Later that week, Jerry saw the animal control truck in front of the Shaw's home. After that, the Shaws tied up their dog in the daytime. They put him in the basement at night.

"Our problem with that dog is over," Jerry said to his wife.

A few nights later, the Dawsons woke up in the dark hours of the morning. "I heard something downstairs," Jean Dawson said to her husband.

"Maybe someone is trying to rob our house," said Jerry. "I'll go down and check it out."

Sure enough, the glass was broken in the kitchen door. Someone had come in. Jerry looked around. The good silver was gone. The silver service left to them by Great-aunt Jane was gone. The silver dollars Jerry had been collecting for years were gone.

Just then, Jerry saw Bob Shaw at the kitchen door.

"What happened?" Bob asked. "I heard something. Then your kitchen light came on, and I saw the broken window."

"Someone broke the glass to open the door," said Jerry. "He was gone by the time I got downstairs, along with most of the silver we owned. I had $2200 in silver dollars alone."

"Well, that's awful. But I was afraid it would happen if we tied up our watchdog," said Bob. "He watches your house as well as mine."

"You could be right," said Jerry. "I was trying so hard to protect my lawn that I put my home in danger. I'm sorry. I acted too fast. We need this dog. Maybe we can have the dog and lawn both—if we put a stronger fence around the lawn."

A Newspaper Story about an Accident

The following story was in the newspaper on the day that Paul Jones had the accident.

Early Morning Traffic Slowed by Tomato Sauce

A three-car accident happened this morning on Highway 66 near Exit 14. A big truck hauling tomato sauce, a laundry truck, and a Ford automobile crashed in the early morning fog. The big truck turned over and the tomato sauce went everywhere. Police who arrived at the accident said they believed at first that the three drivers were badly hurt because they were covered with the sticky, red sauce.

As it turned out, no one was hurt. But early morning traffic was slowed down until the tomato sauce could be cleaned off the highway.

Police said the wet road and heavy fog were two causes of the accident. But they said the driver of the auto was at fault, too, for driving in the fog without lights. Paul Jones, the driver of the laundry truck, said he didn't see the Ford and ran into its rear when it ran across the highway in front of him. Then the big truck behind Jones could not stop on the wet road. In trying to miss the laundry truck, the driver of the big truck ran off the road and turned over. The driver, Dan Oak, drives for Long Haulers out of Porter, Ohio.

No one was hurt in the accident. No one was arrested. But Bud Oliver, who was driving the Ford, was told he was at fault.

Big Numbers in Insurance

billion (bil' yun)	Jackson (Jack' son)
claim	Liberace (Lib er och' ē)
cross	piano (pē an' ō)
desk	property (prop' er ty)
health (helth)	suit (soot)
insure (in shur')	worth (werth)

Insurance is one of the biggest businesses in the country. One company alone has more than $500 billion worth of insurance that it has sold to persons and businesses. (It takes 1,000 million to make a billion.) That insurance company covers life, health, and property. Blue Cross is the biggest health insurance company. In 1983, Blue Cross paid out more than $34 billion for claims.

Life, health, and property are not the only things covered by insurance. Some years ago, a star of moving pictures had her legs insured for $1 million. Most people didn't know that it was because of her insurance that she became "the girl with the million-dollar legs."

Many show people have had themselves and their property insured for a lot of money. Liberace, who played the piano, was one of them. He had a lot to insure: the seven houses he lived in and 15 costly automobiles.

The furnishings in Liberace's home were worth a lot. He insured one old desk for $260,000. The desk was worth so much money because it was owned by a French king in the 1800s. Liberace's pianos, three of which went with him to concerts, were old and well insured.

Liberace played the piano. But part of his act was to wear jeweled suits and many rings on his fingers. He had 200 suits, some worth $25,000, and 400 shirts. He never told how much the clothes and jewels together were insured for. But one time he put in a $500 claim for a jeweled tie that a listener pulled from his neck after a concert.

Rock and roll concerts are just as highly insured as show people's property. Concerts are covered for nearly anything, from property damage to workers being hurt on the job and rock stars not showing up because they're sick or even arrested.

For three to fifteen cents per person, the crowd is insured for things like fights and being robbed. Some outdoor concerts get insurance against rain or high wind.

The average rock concert is insured for $10 million. But some are insured for as much as $50 million. The best protected concerts were those put on by the Jacksons in 1983. The Jacksons paid $2 million for insurance and were covered for more than $150 million.

Maybe you have heard of the Who concert in 1979, when 11 people were killed. They were run over by the huge crowd that tried to crash the gates. More than $2 million was paid to settle the claims. Since then, the people who put on rock and roll concerts have made sure they have enough insurance.

After the Game Was Over

diabetes (dī u bē′ tis)   loss
drug   memorial (mem or′ ē ul)
lose (looz)   Rachel (Rā′ chul)

Jackie Robinson's last year in baseball was 1956. Even then, he was beginning to slow down. But he played in the last World Series that the Brooklyn Dodgers played in.

Two months later, the ball park in Brooklyn was sold. Robinson was sold to another New York team. But because he retired that year, he never played for any team but the Brooklyn Dodgers. The year after he left, the Dodgers moved to California.

Robinson was out of baseball, and he was still in his thirties. He changed from a baseball player breaking records on the playing field to a grey-haired man in a business suit. He also found that he had diabetes.

Diabetes did not stop Jackie Robinson from doing the things he wanted to do. Most of these things had to do with fighting prejudice. His fame as the ball player who broke the color line in major league baseball was bringing him many chances to meet with the nation's leaders and to speak to them. He believed that was the best way to bring about change for the races.

After he retired, Jackie had more time to spend with his family. He and his wife, Rachel, had three children, all still at home. Rachel went back to college, and the children grew up.

Jackie told friends he didn't miss baseball. Even when the old Brooklyn ball park was torn down, he said, "It's no loss to me. People here need apartments more than they need a memorial to baseball."

He did feel a loss in 1965, when Branch Rickey died. "Mr. Rickey's dying is a great loss, not only to baseball, but to America," he told the press.

Jackie was angry that only a few black ball players came to honor Rickey. "Not even flowers," he said, "and they're making all that money." By this time, there were a lot of black players in the major leagues. Robinson believed that Rickey had made it possible.

Not only in baseball, but also in football and basketball, black players had come into their own. Today each of these sports has a Hall of Fame with a growing number of blacks.

Something very sad happened to Jackie and Rachel in 1971. Jackie Robinson Jr. was killed in an automobile accident. He was the son who looked and walked like his father. Young Jackie was only 24 when he died.

Three years before, Jackie Jr. had been arrested for having drugs. It was reported that he had started taking drugs when he was hurt in army duty. After he was cured of taking drugs, Jackie Jr. spent his time helping other young people on drugs.

"You don't know what it's like to lose a son, find him, and lose him again," said the sad father.

Not only was he sad from losing his son, Jackie Robinson was also sick. Diabetes had taken over the strong man. He could no longer drive because he was going blind. Still he pushed for that which was most important to him. In 1972, he went to the World Series and was interviewed on national TV. "I'd like to live to see a black manager in the major leagues," he said. "I'd like to live to see a black man coaching at third base."

Some people found fault with his words. They said he was using the World Series to tell his views to the world. "What better place? What better time?" he asked.

Nine days later, his time had run out. It was October 24, 1972. He was 53.

Most people remember Jackie Robinson as a great baseball player. Rachel Robinson, his wife of 26 years, says she remembers him first as a civil rights leader and then as a ball player.

Calendar of Days to Remember

celebrate (sel' u brate)
Columbus (Col um' bus)
Independence (In dē pen' dens)
Passover (Pass' over)
veteran (vet' er un)

dance (dans)
Easter (East' er)
Eve
leap

In the list below, U.S. national legal holidays are marked with a star (*).

January
1   * New Year's Day
 —   * Martin Luther King's birthday—third Monday

February
 —   * Presidents' Day or Washington's Birthday—third Monday
29   Leap Day comes once every four years because February has 28 days every year but Leap Year.

March
21   First day of spring

April
 —   Easter is the first Sunday following the first full moon after March 21. Easter can come in March or April.
 —   Good Friday comes the Friday before Easter.
 —   Passover comes in April most of the time. Passover lasts for a week.

May
 —   Mother's Day—second Sunday
 —   * Memorial Day—last Monday

June

14 Flag Day

21 First day of summer

—   Father's Day—third Sunday

July

1   Canada Day—celebrates the day in 1867 that Canada became a united nation.

4 * Independence Day

August

—   Rain Dance—Indians of the Southwest dance and ask for rain; they also do the Snake Dance.

September

— * Labor Day—first Monday

21 First day of fall

October

9   Thanksgiving Day in Canada

— * Columbus Day—second Monday. Columbus is remembered as the first white man to find America. Columbus Day celebrates that happening in 1492.

November

11 * Veterans' Day honors the veterans who gave their lives in war. Canada also honors her veterans on this day.

— * Thanksgiving—fourth Thursday

December

21 First day of winter

24 Christmas Eve

25 * Christmas Day

31 New Year's Eve

On the Bus to California

Arizona (Ār iz ō' nu)   Mai (Mī)
desert (dez' ert)   Mommy (Mom' y)
halfway (half way)   Nevada (Nev ad' u)
Los Angeles (Los An' jel es)   orange (or' inj)

Tran Ty Lan was on the bus with her two small daughters. Her father had bought bus tickets for them. They were going to California to live.

Lan felt sad. "I will miss my friend Molly," she said to herself. "I will miss Tom Wong, who might have become more than a friend. I will miss other people in our classroom and the old people at the nursing home."

It had been only two days since Lan and the girls left New York, but it seemed much longer. They had changed buses three times and had come more than halfway across the country. Now they were in Arizona.

"Look, Mommy," said Mai, her younger daughter. "See the pretty rocks. They are red and blue and orange."

"Yes, dear," said Lan. "This part of Arizona is called the Painted Desert. The colors are very beautiful."

"She doesn't know what a desert is," said 9-year-old Kim. "I know because I have seen deserts on TV. A desert is a hot land where it doesn't rain much. There is a lot of sand and not many trees."

"That's right," said Lan. "It is not like our old country. What do you remember about our old country?"

"Our old country was named Vietnam. There was a war in Vietnam. My father fought in that war, and he was killed. That is why we came to live with Grandmother and Grandfather in New York. But why are we going away from them now?" asked Kim.

"Your grandfather thought we ought to live with our relatives in California," said Lan. She went on without thinking that she was talking to her small daughter. "In the old country, a good daughter listened to her father and did what he thought was best. Things are not that way here in the United States. A woman my age can be a good daughter and still think for herself. I still follow the ways taught me in Vietnam. But I see new ways here that seem good. I feel caught between the two worlds."

"You will be OK, Mommy," said Kim. "We will have a good life in California. It's fun to be on the bus and see all the new country. Tell us about it."

"Well, last night while you were sleeping, we went across a state called New Mexico. It is often hot there, like it is here in Arizona," said Lan.

"What other states are we going to see?" asked Kim.

"See this map?" said Lan. "This is Texas. This is New Mexico. This is Arizona, where we are now. Next, we'll cross part of the state of Nevada. And then comes California."

"What will we see in Nevada?" asked Kim.

"More desert, more sand, and a blue, blue sky." said Lan. "See the pictures in this book. We'll be in Los Angeles when you wake up in the morning. It's the biggest city in California. We will not be in Los Angeles long enough to see where the movie stars live. But maybe we can come back later."

"We're going to Roberts to live, aren't we?" asked Kim. "Where is it?"

"My cousin says that Roberts is about halfway between Los Angeles and the capital city," said Lan. "Roberts is in farm country. My cousin says there are orange trees as far as you can see, and then more orange trees. You'll also see tomatoes, beans, and other growing crops."

"Mommy, Mai has gone to sleep," said Kim. "I'll move to the back of the bus so she can sleep better."

"You are a dear girl, Kim," said Lan. "And so is Mai. My father wanted us to go away. But I'm sure he's missing his grandchildren today."

Captain John Smith

captain (cap' tun)
chief (chēf)
England (Ing' glund)
Jamestown (James town)
Pocahontas (Pō' cu hon' tus)

ship
tobacco (tu bac' ō)
Virginia (Vir jin' yu)

Captain John Smith is a name that most Americans know. And most remember that an Indian girl named Pocahontas saved his life. Their story came from the first lasting English town in America.

The town was Jamestown in the part of the New World called Virginia. About 100 men came there from England in 1607.

Captain John Smith was one of seven men picked to lead the Jamestown settlers. He was a young man, 27 years old. He had fought in one war or another for 10 years and had got the title of "captain." That was the only title he could claim, since he was the son of a poor farmer.

The settlers in Jamestown had a very hard time. Indians attacked them. The food ran out because the men did not want to raise crops. They wanted to look for gold. The land was wet, and the drinking water was bad. Many of the men got sick. In four months, 50 of them died. Then Captain Smith was made the only leader.

Smith had the men cut down trees and build a log fort. He had them build log cabins for the coming winter. Some of the men did not want to work because they were of high birth. "He that will not work, shall not eat," the strong young leader said. They worked.

By this time, it was too late to plant a crop. The men were living on fish and wheat with bugs in it. Captain Smith went to the Indians for food.

The Indians gave food for a little while. But they did not want white men to stay on Indian land. "When are you going to go?" asked the old chief.

"When our great captain comes back with big ships, we will go," said the captain.

The Indians did not believe Smith's words. They pushed two great stones before the chief. Then they put Smith's head on the stones. They took up their clubs and were about to kill him.

Pocahontas, the young daughter of the chief, was standing near her father. Her heart was touched by the young white leader. She ran to him and put his head in her arms.

Pocahontas saved Smith's life. The old chief wanted to please his daughter. He would not let the group kill Smith.

After this, in 1608, Captain Smith was made president of Virginia. Two more groups of settlers came to Jamestown. But after a year, Smith was hurt in an accident with a gun. He had to go back to England for care. He never went back to Virginia.

The winter after Smith left Jamestown was a sad time. Without a strong leader in the town, the food was stolen or not given out fairly. When Smith left, there were 490 settlers. Only 60 lived until summer, when another leader came to take Smith's place.

When Smith got back to England, he wrote a book about Virginia. People learned more about Virginia than they knew before. The book told about Pocahontas and how she had saved his life. The English queen asked Pocahontas to visit her in England.

Smith was made captain of another ship going to the New World. This time he went to New England. In fact, that part of the country got its name from what he wrote on his maps. His maps were followed by settlers who came to New England in 1620.

Again, Captain Smith wrote a book about the New World and its riches. "The gold here is in the oceans, rivers, and brooks," he wrote. "The riches are fish, not gold. Any man, woman, or child can pull up money as fast as they can put down a small hook and line."

Captain Smith tried to interest an English company in catching fish in New England waters and taking them to markets in England. That was an idea before its time.

But the town Smith had saved in Virginia did find a way to make money. The Jamestown settlers started tobacco farming. Tobacco became a crop that the settlers could sell. Tobacco sold in England made the settlers richer. (Pocahontas, by the way, married the first tobacco farmer in Jamestown.)

Captain John Smith died in his early fifties. He had helped to name and to settle parts of the New World. He said that Virginia and New England took the place of many things he had never had in life. "They are my children, my wife, my card games," he wrote. He shared that which he loved with the many people who read his books and followed in his steps.

Living with Unemployment

worst (werst)

I'll never forget the year that my husband was unemployed. That year almost destroyed our family. I'm Joyce Johnson, wife of Roy Johnson.

It wasn't Roy's fault that he was laid off at the factory. And his employer had nothing against him. Business was bad all over the country. A lot of employees were laid off.

You would think that Roy would tell his wife what had happened. But no! He went off every morning just like he was going to work. It was three weeks before I found out. Then it was his employer who told me when I tried to call Roy about an emergency. The news that he wasn't working shook me up.

I felt sorry for my husband. But I was angry, too. He should have trusted me enough to tell me the truth. He said he didn't want to worry me. He asked me not to tell our boys. They were seven and nine that year.

So things went on that way for a while. Roy went out every morning looking for a job. He was getting unemployment insurance, and I got a part-time job. That way, we were able to get by.

I wouldn't have found it so bad if Roy had been himself. But somewhere he got the idea that I was disappointed in him. He avoided talking to me or the boys. So he didn't join us for meals.

After a few months, getting a job seemed hopeless to Roy. He stopped looking. Oh, he was out—drinking beer until all hours of the night. Then he would stay in bed all day with the covers over his face. Any little noise the boys made annoyed him. I could see our family being destroyed.

Things went on that way until Christmas week. I knew the holiday without money would be hard on Roy. His unemployment insurance had run out. He was at the lowest point in his life.

I've heard it said that it's good to get to your lowest point—because there's no other way to go but up! That's what happened to Roy. He called us all together and talked about the problem. The boys were so glad to learn what was wrong. They had been afraid that Roy was sick. So a Christmas without many toys didn't seem so bad. They brought out the coins in their savings banks to add to the family money.

That family talk helped all of us. After Roy told the problem to the boys, he went to bed and slept like a baby. When he woke up, he was like a new man. He went out looking for a new job. And he got one! By the end of the year, he was repairing machines at a factory where his friend works.

That year of unemployment was the worst thing that ever happened to our family. Having less money was not the worst part of it. The worst part was having Roy lose his feeling of worth as a man. I'm sure I never measured my husband by the money he brought home. But maybe our way of life supported the idea that a man's worth comes home in a paycheck. We all learned from this experience. I, for one, will always remember that lesson.

I'll go on working. I don't want Roy to feel he has to carry the whole load. And anyway, I enjoy working!

The Job of a Factory Machine Repairer

apprentice (u pren′ tis) repairer
blueprint (blue′ print) tool
break (brāk)

Factories need workers to keep machines in good working order. Sometimes a machine breaks down or doesn't work well. Then the repair person has to work fast. "Down time" costs the factory money because factory workers can't work if the machines are down.

Some of the repair person's time is spent in caring for the machines before they break down. He or she oils and cleans the machines and checks their parts.

In order to repair machines, you have to be able to read machine instruction books and follow the charts in them. You have to be good with machines and know how they work. You have to be able to order the right parts for a machine that is broken down. You may have to keep a record of work that has been done on each machine.

The repair worker has to know how to use hand tools and power tools. The factory furnishes the tools most of the time.

The machine repair worker must be healthy. He or she must be able to lift and to climb. The worker may have to crawl under a machine to repair it or work from the top of a ladder.

What do you have to do to get the job?

Many repair workers start as helpers and learn on the job. Some become union apprentices and learn in a four-year apprentice program. These programs have some on-the-job training and some classroom instructions. Apprentices also get paid while they are learning. High school classes in math and blueprint reading are helpful.

Pay and where the jobs are

Most jobs are in states where there are many factories. The jobs are found mostly in machine shops, printing plants, automobile and airplane plants, clothes and food factories, and oil companies.

Sometimes business is slow, and factories have to close. Often the machine repairer continues to work. That is when some of the big repairs are made on machines.

Repair workers may be called at night or on weekends if there is an emergency. There is often dirt and noise on the job.

Some 421,000 machine repair workers were employed in 1986. The number of jobs will grow more slowly than average up to the year 2000. The average hourly pay for most machine repair workers in 1986 was $8.48 to $12.85.

About Newspapers

product (prod′ uct)

Use one of the following words in each blank. Use each word once.

ads	editors	newspapers	Mon.
advertise	employment	page	sections
apartments	found	possible	Sept.
Aug.	Fri.	products	sports
buy	movies	lost	voice

We read ¹_____ for information and fun. News is on the front page and gives facts on what is happening. The editorial ²_____ is not news. On that page, ³_____ try to get readers to agree with their ideas. We can all have a ⁴_____ in the newspaper through the letters to the editor.

Another section tells about TV shows, ⁵_____, and concerts. You can find news about football, baseball, or basketball games in the ⁶_____ section.

Most of the cost of a newspaper is paid by those who ⁷_____ in the paper. They want the readers to buy ⁸_____ and services. Some people ⁹_____ the paper just to read about the products on sale.

There are ads in all sections of the newspaper. The classified section is different from other ^{10}_____. It has only ads which are classified according to subject. There are ^{11}_____ ads, ^{12}_____ and found ads, and ads about ^{13}_____ for rent.

People try to make their classified ^{14}_____ as short as ^{15}_____. The short form of many words is used. For example, ^{16}_____ is written instead of *September*; ^{17}_____ instead of *August*; ^{18}_____ instead of *Friday*; and ^{19}_____ instead of *Monday*.

Complete sentences are not used in the ads. For example, under Lost and ^{20}_____, the first line might read: "*Cat*—Female, gray" or "*Dog*—Male, black and brown."

The Job of a Bus Driver

cab   route (root *or* rout)
chauffeur (shō′ fer)   trip

The chief duty of a bus driver is to drive a bus safely along a set route. He or she may be taking children to school or passengers to different places in the city. Some bus drivers drive between cities. It is important for the bus to arrive at stops along the route on schedule.

Part of the bus driver's job is to get along with the passengers. They ask questions, both pleasant and unpleasant. Some make rude remarks. The driver usually answers pleasantly. But he or she must stay in control of the bus. Drivers have a lot of independence on the job. Many of them take pleasure in that independence.

Before starting on the bus route, the driver checks out the air pressure in the tires and how much gas there is. A mechanic at the bus company has taken care of any problems found since the last trip.

At each stop, the driver takes on new passengers and collects their money or tickets. Drivers of city and between-city buses make a report at the end of each trip, stating the number of passengers, the money collected, and how well the schedule was kept.

Two out of three bus drivers drive school buses. They usually work part-time, with one or two morning and afternoon routes. Their noon hours are free. They work only when school is going on. They have no work in the summer, or on weekends and holidays. Many women who do not want to work full-time drive school buses.

What you need to get the job

City-to-city bus companies often want their drivers to be 24 years old or older. Twenty-one is the usual lowest age for city bus drivers. Usually, school bus drivers must be 18 or over, but some states let 16-year-olds drive school buses. Usually, drivers must have completed high school.

Most states say a bus driver must have a chauffeur's license. (The chauffeur's license is the one needed to drive cabs and heavy trucks.) Some states have school bus licenses.

To get this job, you must have good sight and hearing. You must have a record of good driving. You must be able to work under pressure. Sometimes, a record of good mental health is needed. You must be able to read and speak English. You must join a union.

Pay and hours

Most school bus drivers work only 20 hours a week. New drivers for city and city-to-city bus companies do not have their own routes. They fill in for older employees. National rules say city-to-city drivers cannot drive more than 10 hours without 8 hours of rest. They average 32 to 36 driving hours a week. City bus drivers usually work a 5-day week with Saturday and Sunday counted as work days.

School bus drivers averaged $8.06 per hour in 1986. City bus drivers working full time averaged $245 to $460 per week. City-to-city drivers averaged $23,500 per year.

Christopher Columbus, Finder of America

Christopher (Chris' tu fer)	round
earth (erth)	ruler
edge (ej)	sail
fail	sailor
India (In' dē u)	sea
mainland	Spain
Portugal (Por' chi gul)	tall

"Sail on! Sail on! Sail on and on!"

The captain was speaking. He and 86 sailors were on three little ships. The men were tired and afraid. They had been on the water for more than two months. There had been no sign of land for 21 days. "Maybe there is no land," the men said to themselves. "Maybe we will fall off the edge of the earth and be killed."

But the captain refused to turn back. He was sure that land was near. As they sailed on, the sea became filled with grass. Then there were many birds. These were signs of land.

The captain and the sailors had been at sea since August 3. On a dark October night, the captain saw a light shining across the water. There was no moon. Was it a star? No, he was sure the light came from land.

Two days later, the shout went up, "Land, land!" The date was October 12, 1492. The captain was Christopher Columbus. He and his men had found America.

Christopher Columbus was not trying to find America. He sailed west from Spain and thought he would come to India. No one had ever followed that route before. People did not try to sail all the way across the Atlantic Ocean. They thought they would fall off the edge of the earth.

Christopher Columbus was born in Italy near the sea. He grew up to be a tall, strong young man with red hair. When he was 22, he went to sea. At that time, no one had heard of America. Maps showed the Atlantic Ocean as the edge of the earth. The Sea of Darkness, as it was called, was full of danger.

A few people believed that the earth was round. Columbus read and sailed. He became more and more sure that the earth was round. He was sure that there was land across the Atlantic.

Columbus left Italy to go to Portugal. In Portugal, he married the daughter of a sea captain. When his father-in-law died, Columbus was given his ocean charts and tools for finding his way on the sea. Columbus studied and thought.

When he was about 30, Columbus started making plans to sail across the Atlantic Ocean. He knew he had to have ships and men. First, Columbus tried to interest his city in Italy, and then the king of Portugal and the king of England. Not one of them chose to help.

At last, Columbus told his ideas to the king and queen of Spain. They were interested, but it took them eight years to get the money. It is said that the queen offered to sell her jewels to pay for the three ships.

*　　*　　*

Columbus and his men went on the shore that October day in 1492. They fell on their knees and thanked God. Then they claimed the land for Spain. They thought they were just off the mainland of India. That's why they called the people there Indians. In truth, they were just off the mainland of Central America.

Columbus left 39 of his men in America to live with the Indians and hunt for gold. He went back to Spain with only two ships. One had crashed on the rocks in America.

Back in Spain, Columbus was given a hero's welcome. The highest honors were given him. The queen made him the ruler of all the land Spain claimed in America. She offered to pay for his next trip there.

Columbus sailed to the New World three more times. On his second trip to America, Columbus had 17 ships and more than 1,000 men. He told the queen that this time he would bring back gold.

Columbus returned to the place where he had left 39 of his men. Less than a year had passed since he left them. The men were all dead. They had been mean to the Indians, and the Indians had killed them.

This time, there was no welcome for Columbus when he returned to Spain. He had left more settlers in the New World. But he had not brought gold, and even the queen was disappointed in him. Still, he made two other trips to America.

Christopher Columbus died in 1506 thinking that he had failed. He had failed to find a route to the Far East. He had failed to find much gold for Spain. He had failed to make the Indians believe in God.

Columbus didn't live long enough to know that he had found a New World. He didn't know that what he found would change all the rest of the world.

Recipe for Mackerel Patties

corn   patties
fork   pepper
mackerel   tablespoon
onion (un' yun)

1. Open 1-pound can of mackerel and remove water.
2. Use fork to cut mackerel into small pieces.
3. Beat one egg with fork, and cut up one onion.
4. Add well-beaten egg and finely-cut onion to mackerel.
5. Sift together and stir in:

   3 tablespoons flour

   $\frac{2}{3}$ cup corn meal

   $\frac{3}{4}$ teaspoon salt

   $\frac{1}{2}$ teaspoon pepper

6. Stir in 3 tablespoons oil.
7. Use hands to form 3-inch patties.
8. Cook in $\frac{1}{2}$ cup hot oil or shortening. Turn to brown on both sides.
9. Serve hot as a snack or for lunch with a salad. Let each person apply hot sauce or more pepper as he likes.

Love Letters in War

gums   waste (wāst)
hate   wheelchair

Medic Gene Bridges was sitting in the army mess tent. He was writing to his wife, Ginger, back in Kansas. Here is what he wrote:

_____

Ginger, my dear wife,

The days go by slowly without you. Even so, I am very busy. Every day, we medics go out where the shooting is and bring in the wounded. We give them first aid, a bandage here and there. But most of them need a lot more than that. Sometimes their screams are awful.

Some don't live until they get to a doctor. Some will have to live without an arm or a leg or spend the rest of their days in a wheelchair.

I can't accept this waste of human lives. As far as I can see, there's no good coming from this war. Our side shoots and kills. Many of the enemy soldiers are just boys. And what do we get from killing them? Sometimes we take over a few more yards of ground. But that's after we have burned it black. Who can use it then?

There is not much difference on the other side. It's all such a waste!

I know I'm telling you more than I ever have about this strange war. I think I'm trying to bridge the distance between us. Lately, Kansas has seemed so far away. You and the baby seem almost like a dream that I had long ago.

I don't like this feeling. This letter is my way of sending myself to you, as I am right now. It may be that someone will black out some of my words. The powers that be don't like for us to find fault with anything here.

It may be that I should write this letter over again, but I don't have the energy. I'm going to rest now and hold you in my thoughts. Take care of our little girl. I love you both.

Gordon Chang was another medic in this war, but he was on the other side. He had not seen his wife, Grace, for almost a year. And he had never seen his six-month-old son.

Gordon was homesick. But most of all, he was sick of war. He hated to hear men cry in pain. He hated to see them die. All that kept him going were the letters from Grace. Below is one that he got on his last day of war.

Dear Gordon,

Next week, we will have been married two years. Mark that occasion on your calendar. I wish we could go dancing together.

Do you remember how we danced on the night you graduated from high school? I shall never forget that occasion. I knew then that we would spend our lives together. Little did I know then that this war would take you from me.

You should see your son. He has two new teeth. Isn't that great? You know it's not easy to cut a tooth. And he let us know it. Your mother and I didn't get much sleep for two nights. Then Mother Chang made a kind of tea from tree bark. She rubbed that on the baby's gums, and it helped. Now he has two beautiful little white teeth in his beautiful little pink mouth.

You have no idea what a handsome boy you have. He has his dad's eyes and nose and his mother's hair and ears. He's not as gentle as you are, but he's almost as sweet. When I lay him down to sleep, he's so quiet and beautiful. I know I'll always have you with me no matter what happens.

I can hear you tell me not to worry. I do try. But until you are back safe in my arms, I am not a whole person. You know that my thoughts and love are with you.

Love always,
Grace

These were the last love letters that Gordon and Gene ever got or wrote.

The Job of a Paramedic

ambulance   paramedic (pār' u med ic)
hospital   patient (pā' shunt)
medical

A new job started in the 1970s. Medical personnel saw how well medics gave emergency medical care to wounded soldiers. It was thought that other persons without a lot of medical training could save lives by giving emergency aid before a patient got to a hospital. This is what the paramedic does.

Paramedics give first aid at an accident or other medical emergency. They arrive in an ambulance or the emergency van of the fire or police department. Two paramedics come together with one of them driving the ambulance.

After they get to the place of the emergency, the paramedics call a doctor at the hospital by two-way radio. They tell the doctor what has happened and get medical instructions. The doctor and the paramedics work together. But since the doctor is at the hospital, and the paramedics are with the patient, they have a standing order to give some first aid without being told to.

Some paramedics work for ambulance companies. Some work for police and fire departments.

What you need to get the job

Paramedics have to be able to think and act in an emergency. They have to be cool and collected and act on short notice under great pressure. They have to want to help people in trouble.

Paramedics have to be strong and healthy. They carry the patient to the ambulance and then into the hospital. Sometimes patients are heavy and have to be carried down flights of stairs.

To be registered as a paramedic, a person has to have 600 to 2,000 hours of training in emergency health care. He or she has to have six months of experience and pass a written test and a skills test.

To be registered as an ambulance driver, a person has to have 80 to 120 hours of training in emergency health care. Both the paramedic and the ambulance driver have to have a chauffeur's license, or one like it, to drive an ambulance.

Police, fire, and health departments offer training programs in emergency health care. So do colleges and medical schools.

Pay and where the jobs are

There are more jobs in fire and police departments than in ambulance companies. Paramedics often work 56 hours a week, some at night, on weekends, or holidays.

Pay is different according to the state and size of the city. Paramedics averaged $18,700 to $24,300 a year in 1987. Beginning ambulance drivers without paramedic training made about half that. Both get paid holidays, health insurance, and savings plans to help them retire.

Studying the Registration Form

longhand

Look at the voter registration form on page 118 of *Skill Book 4.* Circle the letter of the answer that best completes each sentence.

1. On this form, you should
   a. print
   b. write in longhand.

2. Your residence is the place where you
   a. work
   b. go to school
   c. live.

3. The form asks for your
   a. last name only
   b. your first and last names
   c. your first, last, and middle names.

4. The place where you pick up your mail is
   a. your mail order house
   b. your mailing address
   c. your occupation.

5. If you go to school full-time, your occupation is
   a. student
   b. unemployed
   c. citizen.

6. Your present address is the place where you
   a. lived when you registered last
   b. plan to move to
   c. live now.

7. Your employer is
   a. your political party
   b. where you work
   c. the name of your apartment building.

8. If you have citizenship papers, you have to tell a number of things about them. Which information is *not* asked for?
   a. the name of the country you came from
   b. the number on the citizenship papers
   c. the court that issued the papers and the date.

9. On this form, you
   a. have to enroll in a political party
   b. may enroll in a political party
   c. may give money to a political party.

10. The two main political parties in the U.S. are
    a. Social
    b. Democratic
    c. Republican.
    (*Circle two.*)

11. When you write your signature, you usually
    a. write your name in longhand
    b. print your name.

12. You fill out the voter registration form
    a. on Election Day
    b. before Election Day
    c. after Election Day.

Answers: 1-a, 2-c, 3-c, 4-b, 5-a, 6-c, 7-b, 8-a, 9-b, 10-b and c, 11-a, 12-b

The Elephant and the Blind Men

describe (dē scribe′)   tail
upon

Elephants live wild on the land only in Africa and Asia. But elephants have been taken all over the world to be seen in zoos and animal shows. People also know about these unusual animals from books, movies, and TV. Some tales about elephants have been told for many years. This is one such tale.

*   *   *

Once upon a time, four blind men found an elephant and did not know what it was. The only way they could find out was to feel this thing they could not see.

One of the men felt the elephant's leg. The skin was wrinkled and rough. The man wrapped his arms around the leg and felt how thick it was. "This thing is like a log," the first blind man said.

"No, it is like a rope," another of the men said. He had caught hold of the elephant's tail. The tail was made of tough hair. The man thought the tail was like a rope.

The third man was at the other end of the elephant. He ran his hands over the elephant's ears. They were thin and two feet across. The elephant was waving them in the air to keep off the insects. "This thing is like a fan," said the third man.

The fourth man was walking around and around the elephant, feeling its sides. "It is a wall with no beginning and no end," he said.

Each of the blind men described the elephant according to his own experience. They described the animal as a log, a rope, a fan, and a wall. All of them were right. But would anyone know they were describing an elephant?

About Elephants

Use one of the following words in each blank. Use each word once.

African	dumb	limb	thumbs
Asian	heavy	long	trunk
bull	ivory	money	tusks
crumb	knees	pounds	weigh
	knock	things	

A grown male elephant is called a ⁱ_____ elephant. An ²_____ bull elephant may weigh as much as 14,000 ³_____. An ⁴_____ bull elephant may ⁵_____ 12,000 pounds.

The knobs at the end of an elephant's ⁶_____ act as fingers and ⁷_____. The elephant's trunk may pick up something as small as a bread ⁸_____ or as large as the ⁹_____ of a tree.

Although elephants may be called ¹⁰_____ animals, they are not stupid. They can be trained to do many ¹¹_____. Some learn to kneel on their ¹²_____. Some are used as work animals. They can carry ¹³_____ loads. They can ¹⁴_____ down trees by running into them.

Two of the elephant's teeth are very ¹⁵_____. These are the ¹⁶_____. The tusks are made of smooth ¹⁷_____. They can be sold for a lot of ¹⁸_____.

Practicing Health Words

Part A: Fill in each blank with one of the following words.

appointment	clinics	prescription
blood	lab	test
body	non-prescription	throat
chest	nurse	weigh

Getting a physical exam is a way of checking on the health of your ^{1}_____. Some cities have free or low-cost public ^{2}_____ where you can get a checkup. But first you need to call and make an ^{3}_____.

When you arrive for your appointment, a ^{4}_____ will talk with you first. She or he will ^{5}_____ you and measure you. The nurse will also take your ^{6}_____ pressure.

The doctor will look into your eyes, ears, nose, mouth, and ^{7}_____. He or she will listen to your heart and ^{8}_____. The doctor will take some blood for a blood ^{9}_____. He or she may want you to have other ^{10}_____ tests.

If you need medicine, the doctor may write you a ^{11}_____. Or the doctor may tell you to go to the drug store for a ^{12}_____ drug.

Part B: Look at the medicine directions on page 124 of *Skill Book 4*. Circle the letter of the answer below that best completes each sentence.

1. The aspirin dose for an 11-year-old child is
   a. 1 tablet every 2 hours
   b. $\frac{1}{2}$ tablet every 4 hours
   c. 1 tablet every four hours, up to 3 times daily.

2. If people with high blood pressure take cough medicine, they should
   a. take the children's dose
   b. ask a physician first
   c. keep the medicine cold.

3. Cough medicine should not be taken longer than
   a. 24 hours
   b. 1 week
   c. 10 days.

4. First aid spray is to be
   a. taken by mouth
   b. sprayed on minor skin wounds or insect bites
   c. taken as a shot in the arm.

5. The directions warn against using first aid spray
   a. on the head or chest
   b. on a deep wound
   c. on the knees.

6. The directions say to stop using the spray
   a. if redness or pain continue
   b. after you clean the wound with soap and water
   c. after you wrap the wound with a bandage.

Answers: 1-c; 2-b; 3-c; 4-b; 5-b; 6-a.

Graduation at Freedom Center

gotten graduation (graj oo ā' shun)
sang

It was Graduation Day at Freedom Adult Education Center. Forty students were getting their high school diplomas. In addition, thirty students, who had just become new citizens, were being honored.

Gail Newman was one of those getting her diploma. She gave a speech. "Teachers, students, and guests," she said. "I'm speaking for all the students graduating today. Since they can't all speak for themselves, I'll say for us all, 'Thank you! Thank you for making this occasion possible.'

"The decision I made to come here three years ago was the best thing I ever did for myself. My admission to Freedom Center started me on a whole new life. Here's what has made the difference in my life:

"Studying history gave me an understanding of other people and other times, which led to a better understanding of myself. Budget planning, which I studied here, brought improvement to my way of living. Ballroom dancing helped me learn social skills. Of course, my new job is the most important change in my life. It's at the new television station here in Chicago. My job is in the word processing department. I could never have gotten the job without the courses I took here in typing and word processing.

"For myself, and for the other students in this graduating class, I thank you, Freedom Center, and all those that have supported you—and us."

Joseph D'Angelo spoke next. He had just passed his citizenship exams. "I am so proud that I will soon be a United States citizen," he said. "I am so proud that I can stand before you and pronounce English words so that you can understand me. I am thankful to Freedom Center for both of these things."

Helen Baker spoke next. "I'm not getting a diploma or becoming a citizen," she said. "I just want to tell you how much Freedom Center has helped me in my retirement years. The art classes I took here brought me out of my depression after my husband died. Then I took square dancing, where I made some new, great friends. I see they're here tonight. I'm sure I can speak for students over 50 when I say 'Thank God for Freedom Center.' "

After the speeches, the diplomas were handed out. Then it was time for fun. Two students from Italy sang about their mother country. Then everyone sang "This Land Is My Land." A student from Spain did a Spanish dance, and one from Mexico did a hat dance.

Then everyone had a chance to dance to music played by the Freedom Band. Some people danced, but some just ate chocolate chip cookies, along with cold drinks or coffee. Then the party was over, and everyone went home.

Word List

More Stories 4 is correlated to lessons in *Skill Book 4* in the Laubach Way to Reading series. In the list of new words below, variants formed by adding *-s, -es, -'s, -s', -ed, -ing, -er, -est, -y,* and *-ly* to previously taught words are not listed even when *y* is changed to *i* before an ending. New words are listed in their root form when they are used with these previously taught endings. A hyphenated word made from two previously taught words is not listed as new.

Word	Lesson Page/story		Word	Lesson Page/story	
about	12	2-1	claim	54	12-3
afraid	43	9-1	code	21	3-3
amazing	6	1-1	collect	32	5-3
ambulance	83	18-2	collector	32	5-3
apprentice	69	15-2	Columbus	59	13-2
Arizona	61	14-1	control	51	12-1
Arctic	23	4-1	corn	79	17-3
Atlantic	23	4-1	crash	49	10-3
attack	14	2-2	cross	54	12-3
average	9	1-2	dance	59	13-2
basement	30	5-2	danger	38	8-1
because	19	3-2	data	9	1-2
billion	54	12-3	daytime	51	12-1
blue	12	2-1	deliver	35	6-2
blueprint	69	15-2	describe	87	19-1
break	69	15-2	desert	61	14-1
bug	19	3-2	desk	54	12-3
cab	73	17-1	diabetes	56	13-1
captain	64	14-2	diary	28	5-1
celebrate	59	13-2	distance	47	10-2
certificate	35	6-2	dog	43	9-1
chauffeur	73	17-1	drug	56	13-1
chicken	49	10-3	duty	19	3-2
chief	64	14-2	early	38	8-1
Christopher	75	17-2	earth	75	17-2

Word	Lesson Page/story		Word	Lesson Page/story	
east	23	4-1	instruction	9	1-2
Easter	59	13-2	insure	54	12-3
edge	75	17-2	interview	33	6-1
England	64	14-2	Jackson	54	12-3
Eve	59	13-2	Jamestown	64	14-2
experience	35	6-2	land	38	8-1
fail	75	17-2	leap	59	13-2
fireplace	38	8-1	lease	19	3-2
flush	30	5-2	legal	19	3-2
fork	79	17-3	length	47	10-2
fort	38	8-1	Liberace	54	12-3
front	47	10-2	librarian	40	8-2
gas	35	6-2	library	40	8-2
gone	51	12-1	loan	40	8-2
gotten	92	20-1	log	38	8-1
graduation	92	20-1	longhand	85	18-3
gums	80	18-1	Los Angeles	61	14-1
halfway	61	14-1	lose	56	13-1
hate	80	18-1	loss	56	13-1
health	54	12-3	mackerel	79	17-3
heart	14	2-2	Mai	61	14-1
Heimlich	14	2-2	mainland	75	17-2
hello	17	3-1	maybe	51	12-1
homemade	38	8-1	measure	47	10-2
hospital	83	18-2	medical	83	18-2
hour	35	6-2	memorial	56	13-1
how	6	1-1	memory	6	1-1
important	23	4-1	Mommy	61	14-1
inch	47	10-2	Nevada	61	14-1
independence	59	13-2	now	14	2-2
India	75	17-2	ocean	23	4-1
inner	43	9-1	onion	79	17-3
input	9	1-2	operate	9	1-2
inside	38	8-1	operator	9	1-2

Word	Lesson Page/story		Word	Lesson Page/story	
orange	61	14-1	sailor	75	17-2
Ottawa	23	4-1	sang	92	20-1
our	12	2-1	school	9	1-2
out	9	1-2	sea	75	17-2
outside	32	5-3	settler	38	8-1
Pacific	23	4-1	ship	64	14-2
paramedic	83	18-2	shovel	32	5-3
Passover	59	13-2	silver	51	12-1
patient	83	18-2	skill	9	1-2
patties	79	17-3	Spain	75	17-2
payroll	9	1-2	spell	6	1-1
peaceful	28	5-1	step	9	1-2
pepper	79	17-3	subject	40	8-2
personnel	33	6-1	suit	54	12-3
piano	54	12-3	sunny	26	4-2
plaything	38	8-1	tablespoon	79	17-3
Pocahontas	64	14-2	tail	87	19-1
Portugal	75	17-2	tall	75	17-2
pound	49	10-3	tape	9	1-2
power	35	6-2	three-legged	26	4-2
product	71	16-1	tobacco	64	14-2
program	6	1-1	ton	49	10-3
programmer	9	1-2	tool	69	15-2
property	54	12-3	trip	73	17-1
province	23	4-1	upon	87	19-1
Rachel	56	13-1	veteran	59	13-2
receipt	19	3-2	Virginia	64	14-2
reel	6	1-1	wash	35	6-2
repairer	69	15-2	waste	80	18-1
robber	43	9-1	west	23	4-1
round	75	17-2	wheat	23	4-1
route	73	17-1	wheelchair	80	18-1
ruler	75	17-2	worst	67	15-1
sail	75	17-2	worth	54	12-3
			yard	47	10-2